Al-Ma'thurat

THE ULTIMATE DHIKR
COLLECTION FOR
MORNING AND EVENING

Al-Ma'thurat

THE ULTIMATE DHIKR
COLLECTION FOR
MORNING AND EVENING

Hasan al-Banna

1 2 3 4 5 6 7 8 9 10

All rights reserved. No part of this publication may be reproduced, stored in a retrieval system or transmitted in any form or by any means – electronic, mechanical, photocopying, recording or otherwise – without written permission from the publisher.

© Light Publishing 2014

Hasan al-Banna

Al-Ma'thurat

ISBN 978-1-915570-24-6

www.lightpublishing.co.uk

بسم الله الرحمن الرحيم

CONTENTS

Introduction ... 11

Al-Wazifa al-Kubra
Arabic and translation ... 21

Al-Wazifa al-Sughra
Introduction ... 61

Wird al-Rabita
Introduction ... 65

Arabic Appendix I: *Al-Wazifa al-Kubra* ... 69

Arabic Appendix II: *Al-Wazifa al-Sughra* ... 77

Arabic Appendix III: *Wird al-Rabita* ... 83

المأثورات

Al-Ma'thurat

INTRODUCTION

Praise be to Allah, Lord of the worlds. May the peace and blessings of Allah be upon our Prophet Muhammad, the best to perform the *dhikr* (remembrance) of Allah and to give shukr (gratitude), Imam of all the Messengers, the last of all the Prophets and the most renowned leader. May the Peace and Blessings of Allah also be upon his family, his companions and those who follow their rightful path till the Day of Judgement.

1. *Dhikr* at all times

Each human being pursues an ultimate and fundamental goal in life. This goal constitutes one's ideal, the focal point of one's thoughts, aspirations, and activities. The loftier and nobler this goal is, the more sublime are the thoughts and deeds emanating from it.

The basic message of Islam is to elevate the soul,

to purify and uplift it to the highest possible plain. This cannot be accomplished unless Allah is our ultimate goal and the focus of our life. As the Qur'anic verse states: "So flee to Allah. Verily I (Muhammad) am a plain warner to you from Him."[1]

There is no wonder then that the Messenger of Allah ﷺ used to engage in *dhikr*[2] at all times.[3] Following the Prophet's ﷺ example, *dhikr* should be part of our daily life so that one may become closer to Allah: "Indeed in the Messenger of Allah you have a good example to follow for him who hopes in (the meeting with) Allah and the Last Day and remembers Allah much."[4]

ii. Virtues of *dhikr*

Numerous verses of the Qur'an deal with the virtues of *dhikr* and those performing it. Allah says: "For Muslims; men and women, for believing men and women, for devout men and women, for true men and women, for men and women who are patient and constant, for men and women who humble themselves, for men and women who give in charity, for men and women who fast, for men and women who guard their chastity, and for men and women who engage in the *dhikr* of

Allah, for them Allah has prepared forgiveness and great reward."⁵

In another place in the Qur'an, Allah orders the believers: "O you who believe! Remember Allah with much remembrance. And glorify His Praises (in the) morning and afternoon."⁶

There are also numerous ahadith indicating to the virtues of *dhikr*. In a hadith qudsi, the Messenger of Allah ﷺ reported that Allah said: "I (will respond according to) what my servant thinks of Me, and I am with him when he remembers Me. So if he remembers Me in secret, I will remember him in secret and if he remembers Me in a group, I will remember him in a better group."⁷

In another hadith it is reported on the authority of 'Abdullah Ibn Busr that a man went to the Prophet ﷺ and said: "O Messenger of Allah! The laws and conditions of Islam have become too many for me. Tell me something that I can always keep and uphold." The Prophet ﷺ said: "Keep your tongue always moist with the *dhikr* of Allah."⁸

iii. etiquette of *dhikr*

Dhikr is not only limited to words; repentance is *dhikr*, reflection is *dhikr*, seeking knowledge is *dhikr*, seeking lawful provisions (provided that the intention is correct) is *dhikr* and generally, every lawful act during which the presence of Allah is felt is *dhikr*.

For *dhikr* to bear fruit, the following etiquette should be observed:

i. Humility, sobriety and pondering over the meanings of the *dhikr* and the *du'a'*.

ii. Lowering one's voice as much as possible so as not to disturb others but at the same time one must be completely awake. As Allah says: "And remember your Lord by your tongue and within yourself, humbly and with fear without loudness in words in the mornings, and in the afternoons and be not of those who are neglectful (of his remembrance)."[9]

iii. Abiding by the sequence of the group if the *dhikr* is performed collectively. One should not be too fast nor too slow in observing the sequence, but rather keep up with the pace of the group.

iv. Cleanliness and respectability of clothes and the place of *dhikr*.

v. Leaving (the circle of *dhikr*) with khushu

(tranquility) and adab (well-mannered) and thus refraining from excessive talk and jesting that will devoid one of the benefits of *dhikr*.

By observing these guidelines, one will find happiness in his heart, light in his soul and blessings from Allah.

iv. *Dhikr* in a group

Engaging in *dhikr* collectively in a group is permissible. Indeed, it is encouraged in some ahadith. In a hadith the Prophet ﷺ said: "If a group of people sit together remembering Allah, the angels will surround them, the mercy will shroud them, the peace will descend onto them and Allah will remember them among those with Him."[10]

In many other ahadith it can be noticed that the Messenger of Allah ﷺ would pass by a group of companions who were collectively engaged in the *dhikr* of Allah and give them good news and would not condemn them (i.e. their practice).[11]

Engaging collectively in a group in acts of obedience is deemed mustahab (recommended and praiseworthy) as it can lead to many benefits e.g. it brings the hearts of Muslims together, strengthens their noble ties and helps teach others. However if the collective *dhikr* disturbs those who are praying or turns into a gathering full of foolish talk and laughter or the like, then in such circumstances it is not permissible to engage in *dhikr* in a group.

Conclusion

We present this *Wazifa* to the members of the Muslim Brotherhood. However, this is not specific to them but it is for all the Muslims. It should be read individually or in a group in the morning between *Fajr* and *Zuhr*, and in the evening between '*Asr* and '*Isha*'.

We pray to Allah for complete guidance and may the peace and blessings of Allah be upon our master Prophet Muhammad, upon his family and upon his companions.

Hasan al-Banna
Ramadan 1355 A.H.
November 1936, CE
Cairo, Egypt

Notes

1. Surah al-Dhariyat, 51:50.
2. *Dhikr* literally means remembrance. In this specific context, *dhikr* refers to the remembrance of Allah through words, meditation and reflection.
3. 'A'isha (may Allah be pleased with her) said: 'The Messenger of Allah ﷺ remembered Allah at all times.' Related by Muslim, Abu Dawud, Tirmidhi.
4. Surah Al-Ahzab, 33:21.
5. Surah Al-Ahzab, 33:35.
6. Surah Al-Ahzab, 33:42.
7. Related by Bukhari & Muslim.
8. Related by Tirmidhi, Ahmad, Ibn Majah and Ibn Hibban.
9. Surah Al-A'raf, 7:205.
10. Related by Muslim.
11. For example in a narration of Muslim, Tirmidhi and Nisa'i, Mu'awiyah relates that: 'The Messenger of Allah ﷺ went out to a circle of his companions and asked: "What made you sit here?" They said: "We are sitting here in order to remember and mention

Allah and to glorify Him because He guided us to the path of Islam and conferred His favours upon us." Thereupon he adjured them by Allah and asked if that was the only purpose of their sitting there. They said: "By Allah, we are sitting here for this purpose only." At this the Messenger of Allah ﷺ said: "I am not asking you to take an oath because of any misapprehension against you, but only because Jibra'il came to me and informed me that Allah, the Exalted and Glorious, was telling the angels that He is proud of you.'"
[Editor]

الوظيفة الكبرى
Wazifat al-Kubra

(1)

أَعُوذُ بِاللَّهِ السَّمِيعِ الْعَلِيمِ مِنَ الشَّيْطَانِ الرَّجِيمِ

I seek refuge with Allah, the All-Hearer, the All-Knower, from the rejected satan.

(2)

بِسْمِ اللَّهِ الرَّحْمَنِ الرَّحِيمِ ﴿1﴾
الْحَمْدُ لِلَّهِ رَبِّ الْعَالَمِينَ ﴿2﴾ الرَّحْمَنِ الرَّحِيمِ ﴿3﴾ مَالِكِ يَوْمِ الدِّينِ ﴿4﴾ إِيَّاكَ نَعْبُدُ وَإِيَّاكَ نَسْتَعِينُ ﴿5﴾ اهْدِنَا الصِّرَاطَ الْمُسْتَقِيمَ ﴿6﴾ صِرَاطَ الَّذِينَ أَنْعَمْتَ عَلَيْهِمْ غَيْرِ الْمَغْضُوبِ عَلَيْهِمْ وَلَا الضَّالِّينَ ﴿7﴾

In the name of Allah, the Most Gracious; the Most Merciful. Praise be to Allah, the Cherisher and Sustainer of the worlds; the Most Gracious, the Most Merciful; Master of the Day of Judgement. You alone do we worship, and Your help alone do we seek. Guide us to the Straight Path. The path of those whom You have favoured, not of those who have incurred Your wrath nor of those who are astray. (Quran, 1:1-7)

(3)

بِسْمِ اللَّهِ الرَّحْمَنِ الرَّحِيمِ
الم ﴿1﴾ ذَلِكَ الْكِتَابُ لَا رَيْبَ فِيهِ هُدًى لِلْمُتَّقِينَ ﴿2﴾ الَّذِينَ يُؤْمِنُونَ

بِالْغَيْبِ وَيُقِيمُونَ الصَّلَاةَ وَمِمَّا رَزَقْنَاهُمْ يُنْفِقُونَ ﴿3﴾ وَالَّذِينَ يُؤْمِنُونَ بِمَا أُنْزِلَ إِلَيْكَ وَمَا أُنْزِلَ مِنْ قَبْلِكَ وَبِالْآخِرَةِ هُمْ يُوقِنُونَ ﴿4﴾ أُولَئِكَ عَلَى هُدًى مِنْ رَبِّهِمْ وَأُولَئِكَ هُمُ الْمُفْلِحُونَ ﴿5﴾

In the name of Allah, the Most Gracious; the Most Merciful. Alif Lam Mim. This is the Book in which there is no doubt, in it is guidance for those who fear (Allah). Who believe in the unseen, establish the ritual prayer, and spend out of what We have given them. And who believe in that which is sent down to you, and that which was sent down before you, and have certain faith in the Hereafter. They are on true guidance from their Lord, and it is they who are successful. (Quran, 2:1-5)

(4)

اللَّهُ لَا إِلَهَ إِلَّا هُوَ الْحَيُّ الْقَيُّومُ لَا تَأْخُذُهُ سِنَةٌ وَلَا نَوْمٌ لَهُ مَا فِي السَّمَاوَاتِ وَمَا فِي الْأَرْضِ مَنْ ذَا الَّذِي يَشْفَعُ عِنْدَهُ إِلَّا بِإِذْنِهِ يَعْلَمُ مَا بَيْنَ أَيْدِيهِمْ وَمَا خَلْفَهُمْ وَلَا يُحِيطُونَ بِشَيْءٍ مِنْ عِلْمِهِ إِلَّا بِمَا شَاءَ وَسِعَ كُرْسِيُّهُ السَّمَاوَاتِ وَالْأَرْضَ وَلَا يَئُودُهُ حِفْظُهُمَا وَهُوَ الْعَلِيُّ الْعَظِيمُ ﴿255﴾ لَا إِكْرَاهَ فِي الدِّينِ قَدْ تَبَيَّنَ الرُّشْدُ مِنَ الْغَيِّ فَمَنْ يَكْفُرْ بِالطَّاغُوتِ وَيُؤْمِنْ بِاللَّهِ فَقَدِ اسْتَمْسَكَ بِالْعُرْوَةِ الْوُثْقَى لَا انْفِصَامَ لَهَا وَاللَّهُ سَمِيعٌ عَلِيمٌ ﴿256﴾ اللَّهُ وَلِيُّ الَّذِينَ آمَنُوا يُخْرِجُهُمْ مِنَ الظُّلُمَاتِ إِلَى النُّورِ وَالَّذِينَ كَفَرُوا أَوْلِيَاؤُهُمُ الطَّاغُوتُ يُخْرِجُونَهُمْ مِنَ النُّورِ إِلَى الظُّلُمَاتِ أُولَئِكَ

$$\text{أَصْحَابُ النَّارِ هُمْ فِيهَا خَالِدُونَ ﴿257﴾}$$

Allah! There is no god but He, the Living, the Sustainer. Neither slumber nor sleep overtakes Him. His is what is in the heavens and what is in the earth. Who can intercede with Him except by His permission? He knows what is before them and behind them and they can grasp only that part of His knowledge He wills. His Throne embraces the heavens and the earth and it tires Him not to uphold both. For He is the Most High, the Formidable. Let there be no compulsion in religion. True guidance has become distinct from error. But whoever disbelieves in false gods and believes in Allah, has grasped the most strong handhold that will never break. And Allah is Hearing, Knowing. Allah is the Protector of those who believe. He brings them out of the darkness and into light. As for those who disbelieve, their supporters will be false gods, who bring them out of the light into darkness. Such are the dwellers of the Fire, abiding therein perpetually. (Quran, 2:255)

(5)

لِلَّهِ مَا فِي السَّمَاوَاتِ وَمَا فِي الْأَرْضِ وَإِنْ تُبْدُوا مَا فِي أَنْفُسِكُمْ أَوْ تُخْفُوهُ يُحَاسِبْكُمْ بِهِ اللَّهُ فَيَغْفِرُ لِمَنْ يَشَاءُ وَيُعَذِّبُ مَنْ يَشَاءُ وَاللَّهُ عَلَىٰ كُلِّ شَيْءٍ قَدِيرٌ ﴿284﴾ آمَنَ الرَّسُولُ بِمَا أُنْزِلَ إِلَيْهِ مِنْ رَبِّهِ وَالْمُؤْمِنُونَ كُلٌّ آمَنَ بِاللَّهِ وَمَلَائِكَتِهِ وَكُتُبِهِ وَرُسُلِهِ لَا نُفَرِّقُ بَيْنَ أَحَدٍ مِنْ رُسُلِهِ وَقَالُوا سَمِعْنَا وَأَطَعْنَا غُفْرَانَكَ رَبَّنَا وَإِلَيْكَ الْمَصِيرُ ﴿285﴾ لَا يُكَلِّفُ اللَّهُ نَفْسًا إِلَّا وُسْعَهَا لَهَا مَا كَسَبَتْ وَعَلَيْهَا مَا اكْتَسَبَتْ رَبَّنَا لَا تُؤَاخِذْنَا إِنْ نَسِينَا أَوْ أَخْطَأْنَا رَبَّنَا وَلَا تَحْمِلْ عَلَيْنَا إِصْرًا كَمَا حَمَلْتَهُ عَلَى الَّذِينَ مِنْ قَبْلِنَا رَبَّنَا وَلَا تُحَمِّلْنَا مَا لَا طَاقَةَ لَنَا بِهِ وَاعْفُ عَنَّا وَاغْفِرْ لَنَا وَارْحَمْنَا أَنْتَ مَوْلَانَا فَانْصُرْنَا عَلَى الْقَوْمِ الْكَافِرِينَ ﴿286﴾

To Allah belongs all that the heavens and all that the earth contain. Whether you make known what is in your souls or hide it, Allah will bring you to account for it. He forgives whom He will and punishes whom He will; Allah has power over all things. The Messenger believes in what has been sent down to him by his Lord, and so do the believers. They all believe in Allah and His angels, His books and His Messengers: "We make no distinction (they say) between any of His Messengers." And they say: "We hear and we obey. Grant us Your forgiveness, our Lord; to You is the end of all journeys." On no soul does Allah place a burden greater than it can bear. It shall be requited for whatever good and whatever evil it has done: "Our Lord! Condemn us not if we forget or fall into error; Our Lord! Lay not on us a burden greater than we have strength to bear. Pardon us, forgive us, and have mercy on us. You are our Protector; so give us victory over the disbelieving people. (Quran, 2:284-87)

(6)

بِسْمِ اللَّهِ الرَّحْمَنِ الرَّحِيمِ
الم ﴿1﴾ اللَّهُ لَا إِلَهَ إِلَّا هُوَ الْحَيُّ الْقَيُّومُ ﴿2﴾

In the name of Allah, the Most Gracious; the Most Merciful. Alif Lam Mim. Allah, there is no god but He, the Living, the Sustainer. (Quran, 3:1-2)

(7)

وَعَنَتِ الْوُجُوهُ لِلْحَيِّ الْقَيُّومِ وَقَدْ خَابَ مَنْ حَمَلَ ظُلْمًا ﴿111﴾ وَمَنْ يَعْمَلْ مِنَ الصَّالِحَاتِ وَهُوَ مُؤْمِنٌ فَلَا يَخَافُ ظُلْمًا وَلَا هَضْمًا ﴿112﴾

(All) faces shall be humbled before Him the Living, the Sustainer. And he has failed indeed that carries iniquity (on his back). But he who has believed and has done good deeds, shall fear neither injustice nor diminishment (of what is his due). (Quran, 20:111-12)

(8)

حَسْبِيَ اللَّهُ لَا إِلَهَ إِلَّا هُوَ عَلَيْهِ تَوَكَّلْتُ وَهُوَ رَبُّ الْعَرْشِ الْعَظِيمِ ﴿129﴾

Allah is sufficient for me, there is no god but He. In Him I put my trust. He is the Lord of the Formidable Throne. (Quran, 9:129)

(9)

قُلِ ادْعُوا اللَّهَ أَوِ ادْعُوا الرَّحْمَنَ أَيًّا مَا تَدْعُوا فَلَهُ الْأَسْمَاءُ الْحُسْنَى وَلَا تَجْهَرْ بِصَلَاتِكَ وَلَا تُخَافِتْ بِهَا وَابْتَغِ بَيْنَ ذَلِكَ سَبِيلًا ﴿110﴾ وَقُلِ الْحَمْدُ لِلَّهِ الَّذِي لَمْ يَتَّخِذْ وَلَدًا وَلَمْ يَكُنْ لَهُ شَرِيكٌ فِي الْمُلْكِ وَلَمْ يَكُنْ لَهُ وَلِيٌّ مِنَ الذُّلِّ وَكَبِّرْهُ تَكْبِيرًا ﴿111﴾

Say: "Call upon Allah or call upon the All-Merciful; by whatever name you call upon Him, to Him belong the most beautiful Names." Recite (in) your prayers neither too loudly nor too softly, but seek a middle way. And say: "Praise be to Allah, Who has never taken to Himself a son, and Who has no partner in sovereignty. Nor (needs) He an ally to strengthen any weakness." And magnify Him with repeated magnification! (Quran, 17:110-11)

(10)

أَفَحَسِبْتُمْ أَنَّمَا خَلَقْنَاكُمْ عَبَثًا وَأَنَّكُمْ إِلَيْنَا لَا تُرْجَعُونَ ﴿115﴾ فَتَعَالَى اللَّهُ الْمَلِكُ الْحَقُّ لَا إِلَهَ إِلَّا هُوَ رَبُّ الْعَرْشِ الْكَرِيمِ ﴿116﴾ وَمَن يَدْعُ مَعَ اللَّهِ إِلَهًا آخَرَ لَا بُرْهَانَ لَهُ بِهِ فَإِنَّمَا حِسَابُهُ عِندَ رَبِّهِ إِنَّهُ لَا يُفْلِحُ الْكَافِرُونَ ﴿117﴾ وَقُل رَّبِّ اغْفِرْ وَارْحَمْ وَأَنتَ خَيْرُ الرَّاحِمِينَ ﴿118﴾

Did you then think that We have created you in vain, and that to Us you would not be returned? So, exalted is Allah, the King, the True. There is no god but He; the Lord of the Noble Throne. And whoever invokes another god with Allah, of which he has no proof, then his reckoning shall be with his Lord. And verily the disbelievers are never successful. And say: "My Lord! Grant us forgiveness and have mercy, for You are the best of the merciful!" (Quran, 23:115-18)

(11)

فَسُبْحَانَ اللَّهِ حِينَ تُمْسُونَ وَحِينَ تُصْبِحُونَ ﴿17﴾ وَلَهُ الْحَمْدُ فِي السَّمَاوَاتِ وَالْأَرْضِ وَعَشِيًّا وَحِينَ تُظْهِرُونَ ﴿18﴾ يُخْرِجُ الْحَيَّ مِنَ الْمَيِّتِ وَيُخْرِجُ الْمَيِّتَ مِنَ الْحَيِّ وَيُحْيِي الْأَرْضَ بَعْدَ مَوْتِهَا وَكَذَلِكَ

تُخْرَجُونَ ﴿19﴾ وَمِنْ آيَاتِهِ أَنْ خَلَقَكُمْ مِنْ تُرَابٍ ثُمَّ إِذَا أَنْتُمْ بَشَرٌ تَنْتَشِرُونَ ﴿20﴾ وَمِنْ آيَاتِهِ أَنْ خَلَقَ لَكُمْ مِنْ أَنْفُسِكُمْ أَزْوَاجًا لِتَسْكُنُوا إِلَيْهَا وَجَعَلَ بَيْنَكُمْ مَوَدَّةً وَرَحْمَةً إِنَّ فِي ذَلِكَ لَآيَاتٍ لِقَوْمٍ يَتَفَكَّرُونَ ﴿21﴾ وَمِنْ آيَاتِهِ خَلْقُ السَّمَاوَاتِ وَالْأَرْضِ وَاخْتِلَافُ أَلْسِنَتِكُمْ وَأَلْوَانِكُمْ إِنَّ فِي ذَلِكَ لَآيَاتٍ لِلْعَالِمِينَ ﴿22﴾ وَمِنْ آيَاتِهِ مَنَامُكُمْ بِاللَّيْلِ وَالنَّهَارِ وَابْتِغَاؤُكُمْ مِنْ فَضْلِهِ إِنَّ فِي ذَلِكَ لَآيَاتٍ لِقَوْمٍ يَسْمَعُونَ ﴿23﴾ وَمِنْ آيَاتِهِ يُرِيكُمُ الْبَرْقَ خَوْفًا وَطَمَعًا وَيُنَزِّلُ مِنَ السَّمَاءِ مَاءً فَيُحْيِي بِهِ الْأَرْضَ بَعْدَ مَوْتِهَا إِنَّ فِي ذَلِكَ لَآيَاتٍ لِقَوْمٍ يَعْقِلُونَ ﴿24﴾ وَمِنْ آيَاتِهِ أَنْ تَقُومَ السَّمَاءُ وَالْأَرْضُ بِأَمْرِهِ ثُمَّ إِذَا دَعَاكُمْ دَعْوَةً مِنَ الْأَرْضِ إِذَا أَنْتُمْ تَخْرُجُونَ ﴿25﴾ وَلَهُ مَنْ فِي السَّمَاوَاتِ وَالْأَرْضِ كُلٌّ لَهُ قَانِتُونَ ﴿26﴾

So Transcendent is Allah, both in your evenings and your mornings. All praise is His in the heavens and the earth, and at the setting of the sun and in the noonday. He brings forth the living from the dead, and brings forth the dead from the living, and He gives life to the earth after her death. Thus is it that you too shall be brought forth. And among His signs is that he created you from dust behold, you are men scattered (far and wide). And among His signs is that He created for you wives from yourselves that you may dwell in tranquility with them, and He has put love and mercy between your (hearts). Verily in this are signs for those who reflect. And among His signs is the creation of the heavens and the earth, and the variations in your languages and your colours. Verily in this are signs for people of knowledge. And among His signs is your sleep by night and by day, and your seeking of His favour. Verily in this are signs for those who hear. And among His signs is that He shows you the lightning, causing fear and hope, and sends down water from the sky, thereby bringing life to the earth after her death. Verily in this are signs for those who understand. And among His signs is that the heavens and the earth stand firm by His command; then when He summons you, out of the earth you will come. To Him belongs whosoever is in the heavens and in the earth. All are devoutly obedient to Him. (30:17-26)

(12)

بِسْمِ اللَّهِ الرَّحْمَنِ الرَّحِيمِ
حم ﴿1﴾ تَنْزِيلُ الْكِتَابِ مِنَ اللَّهِ الْعَزِيزِ الْعَلِيمِ ﴿2﴾
غَافِرِ الذَّنْبِ وَقَابِلِ التَّوْبِ شَدِيدِ الْعِقَابِ ذِي الطَّوْلِ لَا
إِلَهَ إِلَّا هُوَ إِلَيْهِ الْمَصِيرُ ﴿3﴾

In the name of Allah, the Most Gracious; the

Most Merciful. Ha Mim. The sending down of this Book is from Allah, Exalted in Power, the Knowing. The Forgiver of sins, the Accepter of repentance, the Stern in punishment, the Bountiful. There is no god but He. To Him is the final end. (Quran, 40:1-3)

(13)

هُوَ اللَّهُ الَّذِي لَا إِلَـٰهَ إِلَّا هُوَ عَالِمُ الْغَيْبِ وَالشَّهَادَةِ هُوَ الرَّحْمَٰنُ الرَّحِيمُ ﴿22﴾ هُوَ اللَّهُ الَّذِي لَا إِلَـٰهَ إِلَّا هُوَ الْمَلِكُ الْقُدُّوسُ السَّلَامُ الْمُؤْمِنُ الْمُهَيْمِنُ الْعَزِيزُ الْجَبَّارُ الْمُتَكَبِّرُ سُبْحَانَ اللَّهِ عَمَّا يُشْرِكُونَ ﴿23﴾ هُوَ اللَّهُ الْخَالِقُ الْبَارِئُ الْمُصَوِّرُ لَهُ الْأَسْمَاءُ الْحُسْنَىٰ يُسَبِّحُ لَهُ مَا فِي السَّمَاوَاتِ وَالْأَرْضِ وَهُوَ الْعَزِيزُ الْحَكِيمُ ﴿24﴾

He is Allah besides whom there is no other god; Knower of the visible and the unseen. He is the Most Gracious; the Most Merciful. He is Allah besides whom there is no other god. The Sovereign, the Holy, the Source of Peace (and Perfection), the Guardian of Faith, the August, the Exalted in Might, the Compeller, the Proud. Transcendent is He above what they associate with Him. He is Allah, the Creator, the Originator, the Bestower of forms (or colours). To Him belong the most beautiful Names. Whatever is in the heavens and the earth glorifies Him. He is the Exalted in Might, the Wise. (Quran, 59: 22-24)

(14)

بِسْمِ اللَّهِ الرَّحْمَنِ الرَّحِيمِ
إِذَا زُلْزِلَتِ الْأَرْضُ زِلْزَالَهَا ﴿1﴾ وَأَخْرَجَتِ الْأَرْضُ أَثْقَالَهَا ﴿2﴾ وَقَالَ الْإِنْسَانُ مَا لَهَا ﴿3﴾ يَوْمَئِذٍ تُحَدِّثُ أَخْبَارَهَا ﴿4﴾ بِأَنَّ رَبَّكَ أَوْحَى لَهَا ﴿5﴾ يَوْمَئِذٍ يَصْدُرُ النَّاسُ أَشْتَاتًا لِيُرَوْا أَعْمَالَهُمْ ﴿6﴾ فَمَنْ يَعْمَلْ مِثْقَالَ ذَرَّةٍ خَيْرًا يَرَهُ ﴿7﴾ وَمَنْ يَعْمَلْ مِثْقَالَ ذَرَّةٍ شَرًّا يَرَهُ ﴿8﴾

In the name of Allah, the Most Gracious; the Most Merciful. When the earth is shaken to its (utmost) convulsion, And the earth yields up its burdens, And man says: 'What is the matter with it?' On that day will it declare its news. Because your Lord inspired it. On that day will mankind come forth in scattered groups to be shown their deeds. And he who has done an atom's weight of good will see it, And he who has done an atom's weight of evil will see it. (Quran, 99:1-8)

(15)

بِسْمِ اللَّهِ الرَّحْمَنِ الرَّحِيمِ
قُلْ يَا أَيُّهَا الْكَافِرُونَ ﴿1﴾ لَا أَعْبُدُ مَا تَعْبُدُونَ ﴿2﴾ وَلَا أَنْتُمْ عَابِدُونَ مَا أَعْبُدُ ﴿3﴾ وَلَا أَنَا عَابِدٌ مَا عَبَدْتُمْ ﴿4﴾ وَلَا أَنْتُمْ

عَابِدُونَ مَا أَعْبُدُ ﴿5﴾ لَكُمْ دِينُكُمْ وَلِيَ دِينِ ﴿6﴾

In the name of Allah, the Most Gracious; the Most Merciful. Say: "O disbelievers! I do not worship what you worship, Nor do you worship what I worship. And I shall never worship what you worship, Nor will you ever worship what I worship. To you, your way of life, and to me, mine." (Quran, 109:1-6)

(16)

بِسْمِ اللهِ الرَّحْمَنِ الرَّحِيمِ

إِذَا جَاءَ نَصْرُ اللهِ وَالْفَتْحُ ﴿1﴾ وَرَأَيْتَ النَّاسَ يَدْخُلُونَ فِي دِينِ اللهِ أَفْوَاجًا ﴿2﴾ فَسَبِّحْ بِحَمْدِ رَبِّكَ وَاسْتَغْفِرْهُ إِنَّهُ كَانَ تَوَّابًا ﴿3﴾

In the name of Allah, the Most Gracious; the Most Merciful. When Allah's help comes, and the victory, and you see people enter the religion of Allah in multitude. Then celebrate the praise of your Lord and seek His forgiveness. For He is ever Relenting. (Quran, 110:1-3)

(17)

بِسْمِ اللهِ الرَّحْمَنِ الرَّحِيمِ

قُلْ هُوَ اللهُ أَحَدٌ ﴿1﴾ اللهُ الصَّمَدُ ﴿2﴾ لَمْ يَلِدْ وَلَمْ يُولَدْ ﴿3﴾ وَلَمْ يَكُنْ لَهُ كُفُوًا أَحَدٌ ﴿4﴾

In the name of Allah, the Most Gracious; the Most Merciful. Say: "He is Allah, the One and Only; Allah, the Eternal and Absolute; He has not begotten, nor been begotten. And equal to Him there is none." (Quran, 111:1-4) ✿ REPEAT 3 TIMES

(18)

بِسْمِ اللهِ الرَّحْمَنِ الرَّحِيمِ
قُلْ أَعُوذُ بِرَبِّ الْفَلَقِ ﴿1﴾ مِنْ شَرِّ مَا خَلَقَ ﴿2﴾ وَمِنْ شَرِّ غَاسِقٍ إِذَا وَقَبَ ﴿3﴾ وَمِنْ شَرِّ النَّفَّاثَاتِ فِي الْعُقَدِ ﴿4﴾ وَمِنْ شَرِّ حَاسِدٍ إِذَا حَسَدَ ﴿5﴾

In the name of Allah, the Most Gracious; the Most Merciful. Say: "I take refuge with the Lord of the Daybreak, From the evil of what He has created, From the evil of darkness when it gathers, From the evil of those who blow on knots, And from the evil of an envier when he envies." (Quran, 112:1-5) ✿ REPEAT 3 TIMES

(19)

بِسْمِ اللهِ الرَّحْمَنِ الرَّحِيمِ
قُلْ أَعُوذُ بِرَبِّ النَّاسِ ﴿1﴾ مَلِكِ النَّاسِ ﴿2﴾ إِلَهِ النَّاسِ ﴿3﴾ مِنْ شَرِّ الْوَسْوَاسِ الْخَنَّاسِ ﴿4﴾ الَّذِي يُوَسْوِسُ فِي صُدُورِ النَّاسِ ﴿5﴾ مِنَ الْجِنَّةِ وَالنَّاسِ ﴿6﴾

In the name of Allah, the Most Gracious; the Most Merciful. Say:"I take refuge with the Lord of mankind, The King of mankind, The God of mankind, From the evil of the withdrawing whisperer who whispers in the hearts of Mankind, of jinn and men." (Quran, 113:1-6) ✿ REPEAT 3 TIMES

(20)

أَصْبَحْنَا وَأَصْبَحَ الْمُلْكُ لِلَّهِ،
وَالْحَمْدُ كُلُّهُ لِلَّهِ عَزَّ وَجَلَّ، لَا شَرِيكَ لَهُ، لَا إِلَهَ إِلَّا اللَّهُ،
وَإِلَيْهِ النُّشُورُ. (ثلاثاً)

Morning has risen upon us and sovereignty is all Allah's. Praise is due to Allah alone, He has no partner. There is no god but Him, unto Whom is the return. ✿ REPEAT 3 TIMES

(21)

أَصْبَحْنَا عَلَى فِطْرَةِ الْإِسْلَامِ، وَكَلِمَةِ الْإِخْلَاصِ،
وَدِينِ نَبِيِّنَا مُحَمَّدٍ صَلَّى اللَّهُ عَلَيْهِ وَسَلَّمَ، وَعَلَى مِلَّةِ أَبِينَا إِبْرَاهِيمَ،
حَنِيفًا مُسْلِمًا، وَمَا كَانَ مِنَ الْمُشْرِكِينَ. (ثلاثاً)

We have risen this morning on the innate nature of Islam, on the Word of Sincerity, and on the deen (way of life) of our Prophet Muhammad ﷺ

and on the deen of our forefather Ibrahim, who was a Muslim of true faith and was not an idolater. ✿ REPEAT 3 TIMES

(22)

اللّهُمَّ إِنِّي أَصْبَحْتُ منكَ في نعمةٍ وعافيةٍ وسِترٍ،
فأَتْمِمْ عليَّ نِعمتَكَ وعافيتَكَ وسِترَكَ في الدُّنيا والآخِرةِ. (ثلاثاً)

O Allah! I rise up in the morning with blessing, strength and protection, all of which You have bestowed upon me. So complete Your blessing, the strength (You have bestowed upon me) and Your protection, in this life and in the Hereafter.
✿ REPEAT 3 TIMES

(23)

اللّهُمَّ ما أصبَحَ بي من نعمةٍ، أو بأحدٍ من خَلقِكَ، فمنكَ وحدَكَ لا شريكَ لكَ، فلكَ الحَمدُ، ولكَ الشُّكرُ. (ثلاثاً)

O Allah! Whatever blessing I, or any of Your other creatures, rise up with, is only from You. You have no partner, so all praises and thanks are due to You. ✿ REPEAT 3 TIMES

(24)

يَا رَبِّ! لَكَ الحمدُ كما يَنبغي لجلالِ وجهِكَ،
ولعظيمِ سُلطانِكَ. (ثلاثًا)

O My lord! All praise is due to You as is befitting to Your glorious presence and Your great sovereignty. ✿ REPEAT 3 TIMES

(25)

رضيتُ باللهِ ربًّا، وبالإسلامِ دينًا، ومحمدٍ نبيًّا. (ثلاثًا)

I have accepted Allah as Lord, Islam as a way of life and Muhammad ﷺ as a Prophet and Messenger (of Allah). ✿ REPEAT 3 TIMES

(26)

سُبْحَانَ اللهِ وَبِحَمْدِهِ، عَدَدَ خَلْقِهِ،
وَرِضَا نَفْسِهِ، وَزِنَةَ عَرْشِهِ، وَمِدَادَ كَلِمَاتِهِ. (ثلاثًا)

Glory be to Allah and praise is His (as great as) the number of His creatures, the extent of His satisfaction, the weight of His domain, and the ink (needed to write down His countless) signs. ✿ REPEAT 3 TIMES

(27)

بِسْمِ اللهِ الذي لا يَضُرُّ مع اسمِهِ شيءٌ
في الأرضِ ولا في السـماءِ وهو السـميعُ العليمُ. (ثلاثاً)

In the Name of Allah, with Whose Name nothing on earth or in heaven can cause any harm and He is the All-Hearer, the All-Knower. ✿ REPEAT 3 TIMES

(28)

اللَّهُمَّ إنَّا نَعوذُ بك مِن أنْ نُشرِكَ بك شيئًا نَعلَمُه،
ونَستغفِرُكَ لِما لا نَعلَمُ. (ثلاثاً)

O Allah! We seek Your protection from knowingly associating others with You and we seek Your forgiveness from associating others with You unknowingly. ✿ REPEAT 3 TIMES

(29)

أَعوذُ بكلِمَاتِ اللهِ التَّامَّاتِ مِن شَرِّ ما خَلَقَ. (ثلاثاً)

I seek refuge in the perfect words of Allah from the evil of that which He has created. ✿ REPEAT 3 TIMES

(30)

اللَّهُمَّ إنِّي أَعوذُ بكَ مِنَ الهَمِّ والحَزَنِ، والعَجْزِ والكَسَلِ، والجُبْنِ

والبُخْلِ، وَضَلَعِ الدَّيْنِ، وغَلَبَةِ الرِّجالِ. (ثلاثًا)

O Allah! I seek Your protection from anxiety and sorrow, and I seek Your protection from helplessness and laziness, and I seek Your protection from cowardice and miserliness, and I seek Your protection from the burden of debts and the tyranny of men. ✿ REPEAT 3 TIMES

(31)

اللهمَّ عافِني في بدَني، اللهمَّ عافِني في سمعي،
اللهمَّ عافِني في بصري، اللهمَّ إنِّي أعوذُ بكَ مِنَ الكفرِ والفقرِ،
اللهمَّ إنِّي أعوذُ بِكَ مِنَ عذابِ القبرِ، لا إلَهَ إلَّا أنتَ. (ثلاثًا)

O Allah! Grant health to my body. O Allah! Grant health to my hearing. O Allah! Grant health to my sight. ✿ REPEAT 3 TIMES

(32)

اللهمَّ إنِّي أعوذُ بِكَ مِنَ الكفرِ والفقرِ،
اللهمَّ إنِّي أعوذُ بِكَ مِنَ عذابِ القبرِ، لا إلَهَ إلَّا أنتَ. (ثلاثًا)

O Allah! I seek Your protection from disbelief and poverty, and I seek Your protection from the punishment of the grave. None has the right to be worshipped except you. ✿ REPEAT 3 TIMES

(33)

اللَّهُمَّ أَنْتَ رَبِّي، لَا إِلَهَ إِلَّا أَنْتَ، خَلَقْتَنِي وَأَنَا عَبْدُكَ، وَأَنَا عَلَى عَهْدِكَ وَوَعْدِكَ مَا اسْتَطَعْتُ، أَبُوءُ لَكَ بِنِعْمَتِكَ عَلَيَّ، وَأَبُوءُ لَكَ بِذَنْبِي فَاغْفِرْ لِي، فَإِنَّهُ لَا يَغْفِرُ الذُّنُوبَ إِلَّا أَنْتَ. (ثلاثاً)

O Allah! You are my Lord, there is no god but You. You created me and I am your slave, and I uphold Your pledge and promise as best as I can. I seek Your protection against the evil that I have committed. I acknowledge Your blessing upon me and I acknowledge my sin. So forgive me, for none can forgive sins except You. ✿ REPEAT 3 TIMES

(34)

أَسْتَغْفِرُ اللَّهَ الَّذِي لَا إِلَهَ إِلَّا هُوَ الحَيُّ القَيُّومُ وَأَتُوبُ إِلَيْهِ. (ثلاثاً)

I seek forgiveness from Allah, none has the right to be worshipped except Him, the Living, the Eternal and I repent to Him. ✿ REPEAT 3 TIMES

(35)

اللَّهُمَّ صَلِّ عَلَى مُحَمَّدٍ، وَعَلَى آلِ مُحَمَّدٍ، كَمَا صَلَّيْتَ عَلَى إِبْرَاهِيمَ، وَعَلَى آلِ إِبْرَاهِيمَ، إِنَّكَ حَمِيدٌ مَجِيدٌ، وَبَارِكْ عَلَى مُحَمَّدٍ، وَعَلَى آلِ

AL-MA'THURAT

مُحَمَّدٍ، كَمَا بَارَكْتَ عَلَى إِبْرَاهِيمَ، وَعَلَى آلِ إِبْرَاهِيمَ، فِي الْعَالَمِينَ إِنَّكَ حَمِيدٌ مَجِيدٌ. (عشراً)

O Allah! Exalt and have mercy on Muhammad and on the family of Muhammad as You had mercy on Ibrahim and on the family of Ibrahim. And bless our master Muhammad and the family of our master Muhammad as You blessed our master Ibrahim and the family of our master Ibrahim in this universe. Indeed, You are Gracious, Glorious.

✿ REPEAT 10 TIMES

(36)

سُبْحَانَ اللهِ، وَالْحَمْدُ لِلَّهِ، وَلَا إِلَهَ إِلَّا اللهُ، وَاللهُ أَكْبَرُ. (مائة)

Glory be to Allah; Praise is due to Allah; there is no god but Allah and Allah is the greatest.

✿ REPEAT 100 TIMES

(37)

لا إِلَهَ إِلَّا اللَّهُ وحْدَهُ لا شَرِيكَ له،
له المُلْكُ وله الحَمْدُ، وهو على كُلِّ شيءٍ قَدِيرٌ. (عشراً)

There is no god but Allah alone. He has no partner. Sovereignty and Praise are His; and He is

Omnipotent. ✿ REPEAT 10 TIMES

(38)

سـبحانَكَ اللّهمَّ وبحمدِكَ أشهدُ أن
لا إلهَ إلّا أنتَ أسـتغفرُكَ وأتوبُ إليكَ. (ثلاثاً)

Glory and all Praise be to you O Allah! I testify that there is no god but You. I seek Your forgiveness and to You do I repent. ✿ REPEAT 3 TIMES

(39)

اللهمَّ صلِّ وسـلِّمْ وبارِكْ على سيِّدنا محمَّد،
عبدك ونبيِّك ورسولك النبيِّ الأُمّي، وعلى آله وصحْبه وسـلِّمْ
تسليمًا؛ عـددَ ما أحاط به علمُك، وخطَّ به قلمُك، وأحصاه كتابُك،
وارضَ اللهمَّ عن سـادتنا أبي بكر وعمر، وعثمان وعلي، وعن
الصحابةِ أجمعين، وعن التابعين وتابعيهم بإحسـانٍ إلى يوم الدِّين.

O Allah! Exalt our master Muhammad, Your servant, Your Prophet, Your Messenger, the unlettered Prophet and on his family and companions. Give perfect salutation, as much as Your knowledge surrounds, and as much as Your pen wrote and as much as Your book counted. O Allah! Be pleased with our masters - Abu Bakr, Umar, 'Uthman and Ali and all the companions and their followers and those who came after them (on their way) in benevolence till the day of Judgement.

(40)

سُبْحَانَ رَبِّكَ رَبِّ الْعِزَّةِ عَمَّا يَصِفُونَ
وَسَلَامٌ عَلَى الْمُرْسَلِينَ وَالْحَمْدُ لِلَّهِ رَبِّ الْعَالَمِينَ

Glory be to You O Lord! The Lord of Honour and Power who He is free from what they ascribe to Him. May peace be upon the Messengers and all praise is due to Allah, the Lord and Sustainer of the worlds.

*When reading the *Wazifa* in the evening, take note of the following changes:

1. Instead of أَصْبَحْنَا read أَمْسَيْنَا
2. Instead of أَصْبَحْتُ read أَمْسَيْتُ
3. Instead of أَصْبَحَ read أَمْسَى
4. Instead of النُّشُورُ read الْمَصِيرُ

Notes

1. Allah the Exalted says: "And when you recite the Qur'an, seek refuge with Allah from the rejected satan." (Surah Al-Nahl: v. 98). Anas a eported that the Messenger of Allah ﷺ said: "Whoever says when he rises up in the morning: 'I seek refuge with Allah, the All-Hearer, the All-Knower from the rejected satan' will be protected from the satan till evening." Related by Ibn Sunni.

2. Ubay Ibn Ka'b a reported that the Messenger of Allah ﷺ said: "By Him in Whose Hand my soul is, nothing like it was revealed in the Torah, Gospel, Psalms, or the Furqan. It is the seven oft-repeated verses and the Formidable Qur'an which I have been given." Related by Tirmidhi.

3. Ibn Mas'ud ﷺ reported that the Messenger of Allah ﷺ said: "Whoever recites ten verses from Surah Al-Baqarah in the early morning, satan will not get near him until evening approaches; and if it is read when the evening has entered, satan will not get near him until he rises up in the morning. He will (also)

see nothing he dislikes in his family and his wealth." Related by Bayhaqi.

4. Ubay Ibn Ka'b ؓ reported that the Messenger of Allah ﷺ once asked: "Abul Mundhir, do you know which verse of the Book of Allah that you have is the greatest?" I replied: 'Allah and His Messenger know best.' He repeated his question and I said: 'Allah, there is no God but He, the Living, the Sustainer ?' Thereupon he struck me on the breast saying: 'May knowledge be your delight, O Abul Mundhir!'" Related by Muslim.

5. Abu Mas'ud ؓ reported that the Messenger of Allah ﷺ said: "If anyone recites the last two verses of Surah Al-Baqarah at night, they will avert harm from him." Related by Tirmidhi.

6. Al-Qasim Ibn 'Abd al-Rahman ؓ reported that the Messenger of Allah ﷺ said: "Allah's greatest name can be found in three surahs: Al-Baqarah, Al-'Imran and Taha." Sa'id Qasim: "I found it in the verse of the Throne and it is Al-hayy and Al-Qayyum." Related by Hakim.

7. Abu Darda' ؓ reported that the Messenger of Allah ﷺ said: "Whoever recites 'Allah is suf-

ficient for me, there is no god but He and in Him is my trust. He is the Lord of the Great Throne' seven times in the morning and in the evening, Allah will protect his interests in this world and in the life hereafter." Related by Abu Dawud.

8. Abu Musa Al-Ash'ari ﷺ reported that the Messenger of Allah ﷺ said: "Whoever recites these verses in the morning and the evening, his heart will not die that day or that night." Related by Daylami.

9. Muhammad Ibn Ibrahim Al-Taymi narrates that his father said: "The Messenger of Allah ﷺ sent us on a military campaign and commanded us to read these verses in the morning and in the evening. We read them and we were blessed with success and protection." Related by Ibn Sunni.

10. Ibn 'Abbas ﷺ reported that the Messenger of Allah ﷺ said: "Whoever recites these verses in the morning will have obtained that which he had missed the previous day and whoever recites these verses in the evening will have obtained whatever he has missed out at night." Related by Abu Dawud.

AL-MA'THURAT

11. Abu Hurayrah ؓ reported that the Messenger of Allah ﷺ said: "Whoever recites these verses and Ayatul Kursi when he rises in the morning he will be protected till the evening and whoever recites these verses in the evening will enjoy the protection (of Allah) till the morning." Related by Tirmidhi

12. Abu Umamah ؓ reported that the Messenger of Allah ﷺ said: "Anyone who reads the last verses of Al-Hashr in the day or in that night, Allah will take responsibility for that person to enter Paradise." Related by Bayhaqi.

13. Ma'qal Ibn Yasar ؓ reported that the Messenger of Allah ﷺ said: "Whoever recites these verses in the morning and in the evening, Allah will order the angels to pray for such a person during that day or night." Related by Darmi.

14. Ibn 'Abbas ؓ reported that he heard the Messenger of Allah ﷺ saying that this surah equals half of the Qur'an. Related by Tirmidhi.

15. Ibn 'Abbas ؓ reported that he heard the Messenger of Allah ﷺ saying that this surah is equal to one fourth of the Qur'an. Related by Tirmidhi.

16. Anas Ibn Malik ﷺ reported that the Messenger of Allah ﷺ said to one of his companions: "Do you have (Surah) Al-Nasr with you?" He replied: "Yes". The Messenger of Allah ﷺ said: "It is one fourth of the Qur'an." Related by Tirmidhi.

17. Abu Hurayra ﷺ reported that the Messenger of Allah ﷺ declared this surah as equal to one third of the Qur'an. Related by Tirmidhi. Anas Ibn Malik ﷺ reported that a person said to the Messenger of Allah ﷺ that he loves this surah. The Messenger of Allah ﷺ said: "Your love for this surah will take you to Paradise." Related by Tirmidhi.

18. & 19. Abdullah Ibn Khubayb ﷺ said: "Once we went out on a dark and rainy night looking for the Messenger of Allah ﷺ in order to pray with him. We found him and he said: 'Read!' I did not say anything. He then said: 'Read!' and I did not say anything. He repeated again: 'Read!', so I asked him: 'What shall I read?' The Messenger of Allah ﷺ replied: 'Read Surah Al-Ikhlas, Surah Al-Falaq and Surah Al-Nas three times in the morning and in the evening. It will make you suffi-

cient of everything (i.e. your requirements will ne fulfilled)." Related by Tirmidhi.

20. Abu Hurayrah ﷺ said: 'The Messenger of Allah ﷺ when he rose in the morning, used to say: "Morning has risen upon us and sovereignty is all Allah's. Praise is due to Allah alone, He has no partner. There is no god but Him, unto Whom is the return." When the evening approaches, he used to say: "Evening has fallen upon us and sovereignty is all Allah's. Praise is due to Allah alone, He has no partner. There is no god but Him, unto Whom is the return." Related by Ibn Sunni and Bazzar.

21. Ubay Ibn Ka'b ﷺ said that 'the Messenger of Allah ﷺ taught us to say when we rise in morning: "We have risen this morning on the innate nature of Islam, on the Word of Sincerity, and on the deen (way of life) of our Prophet Muhammad ﷺ and on the deen of our forefather Ibrahim, who was a Muslim and of true faith and was not an idolater" and to say the same when one reaches the evening.' Related by 'Abdullah Ibn Imam Ahmad in his *Zawa'id*.

22. Ibn 'Abbas ؓ narrated that the Messenger of Allah ﷺ said: "Whosoever says three times when he wakes up in the morning and when he reaches the evening, 'O Allah! I rise up in the morning with blessing, strength, and protection; all of which You have bestowed upon me. So complete Your blessing and the strength (You have bestowed upon me) and Your protection, in this life and in the Hereafter,' it will become a right upon Allah to complete His blessings upon him." Related by Ibn Sunni.

23. 'Abdullah Ibn Ghanam Al-Bayadi ؓ narrated that the Messenger of Allah ﷺ said: "Whosoever says when he wakes up in the morning: 'O Allah! Whatever blessing I or any of Your other creatures rise up with, is only from You. You have no partner, so all praises and thanks are due to You' has fulfilled his (duty of) thanks (to Allah) for the day; and the one who says the same when evening arrives has fulfilled his (duty of) thanks (to Allah) for the night." Related by Abu Dawud, Nisa'i and Ibn Hibban.

24. 'Abdullah Ibn 'Umar ؓ narrated that the

Messenger of Allah ﷺ spoke to them about a servant from amongst the servants of Allah who said: 'O my Lord! All praise is due to You which is befitting Your glorious presence and Your great sovereignty', and this became problematic between two angels, for they did not know how to write it. They ascended to the Heavens and said: 'O our Lord! Your servant has said something that we do not know how to write?' Allah said and He is the Most Knowledgeable about what His servant has said: 'What has My servant said?' They replied: 'O Lord! He said: 'O my Lord! All praise is due to You which is befitting Your glorious presence and Your great sovereignty.'" Thereon Allah said to them: 'Write it down as my servant has said it so that when he meets Me, I will give the reward for it.' Related by Imam Ahmad and Ibn Majah.

25. Abu Sullam ؓ narrated that the Messenger of Allah ﷺ said: "The one who says, when he wakes up in the morning and when evening arrives: 'I have accepted Allah as Lord, Islam as a way of life and Muhammad as a Prophet and Messenger', it will become a right upon

Allah to please him and accept him." Related by Abu Dawud, Tirmidhi, Nisa'i and Hakim.

26. Juwayriyah, mother of the Believers j, narrated that once the Messenger of Allah ﷺ went out of his apartment when she was offering the Morning Prayer. When he came back in the forenoon, she was still sitting there. Observing this, he said: "I recited four words three times after I left you and if these were to be weighed against what you have recited since morning then these would outweigh them: 'Glory be to Allah and praise is His (as great as) the number of His creatures, the extent of His satisfaction, the weight of His domain, and the ink (needed to write down His countless) signs (of presence, omnipotence, and grace).'" Related by Muslim.

27. 'Uthman Ibn Affan ؓ narrated that the Messenger of Allah ﷺ said: "The servant who says in the morning of every day and in the evening of every night: 'In the Name of Allah, with Whose Name nothing on earth or in heaven can cause any harm, and He is the All-Hearer, the All-Knower', three times, nothing will cause him any harm. Related by

Abu Dawud and Tirmidhi.

28. Abu Musa Al-Ash'ari ؓ narrates that the Messenger of Allah ﷺ addressed them one day saying: "O people! Fear this shirk as it is more concealed than an ant in the darkness of the night." Then somebody said to him: "How can we fear it if it is more concealed than an ant in the darkness of the night, O Messenger of Allah?" He said: "Say: 'O Allah! We take refuge with You from knowingly associating others with You and we seek Your forgiveness from associating others with You unknowingly.'" Related by Ahmad and Tabarani.

29. Abu Hurayrah ؓ narrated that the Messenger of Allah ﷺ said: "The one who says when evening arrives: 'I seek refuge in the perfect words of Allah from the evil of that which he has created', three times, then not even the poison would harm him that night." Related by Ibn Hibban.

30. Abu Sa'id Al-Khudri ؓ narrated that one day the Messenger of Allah ﷺ entered the mosque and found a man from the Ansar, named Abu Umamah. He said: "O Abu Umamah! Why do I see you sitting in the mosque outside

the time of prayer?" Abu Umamah replied: "Anxieties and debts have remained with me." The Messenger of Allah ﷺ asked: "Should I not teach you words, which if you say Allah will remove your anxiety and will settle your debt?" He replied: "Definitely, O Messenger of Allah s." He said: "Say when you wake up in the morning and when you reach the evening: 'O Allah! I seek Your protection from anxiety and sorrow, and I seek Your protection from helplessness and laziness, and I seek Your protection from cowardice and miserliness, and I seek Your protection from the burden of debts and from the tyranny of men.' Abu Umamah said (later): "I did (as the Messenger of Allah ﷺ said) and Allah removed my anxiety and settled my debt." Related by Abu Dawud.

31. & 32. 'Abd al-Rahman Ibn Abi Bakrah ﷺ narrated that he said to his father: "O my father! I hear you pray every morning: 'O Allah! Grant health to my body. O Allah! Grant health to my hearing. O Allah! Grant health to my sight. O Allah! I seek Your protection from disbelief and poverty, and I seek Your protection from the punishment of the

AL-MA'THURAT

grave. None has the right to be worshipped except You.' You repeat it three times when you wake up in the morning and three times when you reach the evening?" Abu Bakrah said: "I heard the Messenger of Allah ﷺ pray with it and I wish to abide by his sunnah." Related by Abu Dawud.

33. Shaddad Ibn Aws ؓ narrated the Messenger of Allah ﷺ said: "The best of istighfar (seeking forgiveness) is (to say): 'O Allah! You are my Lord, there is no god but You. You created me and I am your slave, and I uphold Your pledge and promise as best as I can. I seeMk Your protection against the evil that I have done. I acknowledge Your blessing upon me and I acknowledge my sin. So forgive me, for none can forgive sins except You.' Whosoever says it in the evening with firm conviction and then dies in that night, will enter Paradise." Related by Bukhari.

34. Zayd ؓ the *mawla* of the Messenger of Allah ﷺ said: "I heard my father say on the authority of my grandfather that he heard the Messenger of Allah ﷺ say: "Whosoever says: 'I seek forgiveness from Allah, none has the

right to be worshipped except Him, the Living, the Eternal and I repent to Him', will be forgiven even if he escaped from the advance of an army (in *Jihad*)." Related by Abu Dawud, Tirmidhi and Hakim.

35. Abu Darda' 🙦 narrated that the Messenger of Allah 🙐 said: "Whosoever invokes blessings onto me when he wakes up in the morning ten times and ten times when he reaches the evening, my intercession will reach him on the Day of Judgement." Related by Tabarani.

36. 'Amr Ibn Shu'ayb, on the authority of his father and his grandfather narrated that the Messenger of Allah 🙐 said: "Whosoever glorifies Allah a hundred times in the early morning, and a hundred times in the evening, will be (receiving the reward) of the one who performed a hundred hajj. Whosoever praises Allah a hundred times in the early morning and a hundred times in the evening, will be like the one who brings a hundred horses in the path of Allah (in Jihad), or he will be like the one who fought in a hundred battles. Whosoever says la ilaha illal llah a hundred times in the early morning

and a hundred times in the evening, will be like the one who has freed a hundred slaves from the children of Ismail. And whosoever exalts Allah a hundred times in the early morning and a hundred times in the evening, no one will come that day doing more that what he has done, except the one who says what he has said or has said more than he has said." Related by Tirmidhi and Nisa'i.

Umm Hani, may Allah be pleased with her, narrated that the Messenger of Allah ﷺ said: "O Umm Hani! If you wake up in the morning, glorify Allah one hundred times (*tasbih*); say la ilaha illa llah a hundred times (*tahlil*); praise Him a hundred times (*hamd*); exalt Him a hundred times (*takbir*). A hundred tasbih is like giving a hundred mountain goats as a gift, and a hundred tahlil will ensure that there will be no sin (left recorded) before it or after it." Related by Tabarani.

37. Abu Ayyub ﷺ narrated that the Messenger of Allah ﷺ said: "Whosoever says when he wakes up in the morning: 'There is no god but Allah alone. He has no partner. Sovereignty and Praise are His; and He is Omnip-

otent', ten times; Allah will write for each one said ten hasanat (rewards) and will reduce ten sayyiat (punishable acts performed), and will raise him ten stages higher. The same is also for the one says it in the evening." Related by Ahmad and Tabarani.

38. Jubayr Ibn Mut'am ؓ narrated that the Messenger of Allah ﷺ said: "Whosoever says: 'Glory be to you, O Allah, and all Praise! I testify there is no god but You. I seek Your forgiveness and to You do I repent', in a circle of *dhikr*; he will verily be rewarded by it and whosoever says it in a circle of idle talk; it will redeem him from that (act of disobedience)." Related by Nisa'i, Tabarani and Hakim.

39. & 40. Imam Al-Nawawi has reported a narration from 'Ali ؓ where he says: "He who likes to get a full measure (of reward) should say 'Glory be to You O Lord, the Lord of Honour and Power who is free from what they ascribed to Him. May Peace be upon the Messengers and all Praise is due to Allah, the Lord and Sustainer of the worlds.'" Narrated in the *Adhkar* of Imam Al-Nawawi.

الوظيفة الصغرى

Al-Wazifa al-Sughra

INTRODUCTION TO
Al-Wazifa al-Sughra

If one does not have sufficient time to complete or read the complete *Wazifa*, he should summarise it as follows: He should read the Isti'adhah (1), *Fatiha* (2), *Ayatul Kursi* (3), the last verses of *Surah Al-Baqarah* (4), *Surah Al-Ikhlas* (17), *Surah Al-Falaq* (18), *Surah Al-Nas* (19); each and every one three times. This is to be followed by the mentioned adhkar until the last *istighfar*: 'I seek forgiveness from Allah, none has the right to be worshipped except Him, the Living, the Eternal and I repent to Him' (34). Immediately following which, he should continue from: 'Glory and all Praise be to You, O Allah! I testify there is no god but You. I seek Your forgiveness and to You do I repent' (38), till the end.

This version of the *Wazifa* is known as *'Al-Wazifa al-Sughra*. (For the Arabic text, see Appendix II.)

ورد الرابطة

Wird al-Rabita

INTRODUCTION TO
Wird al-Rabita

Wird al-Rabita is a litany taken from the fourth section of *Al-Ma'thurat*. It is an affirmation of the brotherhood that exists between the believers and aims to strengthen the spiritual bond between them. Imam Hasan al-Banna composed this *wird*, the prime focus of which is the hearts of those who are striving to establish the *dhikr* of Allah in all spheres of life. The *wird* may be classified as follows: 'O Allah you know that these hearts have come together:'

Characteristics of the Hearts
1. Gathered in the love of Allah.
2. Meeting together in the obedience of Allah.
3. United for Allah's Message.
4. Entered into a Covenant to establish Allah's Shari'ah.

Training of the Hearts
1. Strengthen the brotherhood between the hearts.
2. Make permanent the affection between them.
3. Guide them to their path.

Provision of the Hearts
1. Fill them with the Light of Allah that never diminishes.
2. Comfort their hearts with the abundance of faith.
3. Fill them with complete trust in Allah.

Function of the Hearts
1. Keep them alive with knowledge of Allah.
2. Give them their death in martyrdom for the sake of Allah.

Again, this is known as *Wird al-Rabita*. (See Appendix iii for the Arabic text of this *wird*. The translation follows.)

Say: "O Allah, Lord of Power and Rule, You give power to whom You will and You take away power from whom You will. You exalt whom You will and abase whom You will. In Your Hand lies all that is good. Over all things You have power. You cause the night to pass into the day and You cause the day to pass into the night. You bring forth the living from the dead and the dead from the living. And You give sustenance to whom You will, without any measure.

One should then recite the following *du'a'*:

O Allah, this is the coming of Your night, the turning away of Your day and the voices of the callers to You. So forgive Me.

The reader should then recall into his mind all of his brothers that he knows, raise his awareness of the spiritual bond that he has with the ones that he does not know, and pray for all with the following *du'a'*:

O Allah! You know that these hearts have come together in loving You, met together in Your obedience, united for Your message and entered together into a covenant to support Your Way. O Allah! Strengthen the bond between these hearts, make permanent the affection between them, guide them to their paths, fill them with Your Light that never diminishes, comfort their hearts with abundance of faith in You and complete trust in You, keep them alive with knowledge of You and give them their death in martyrdom for You. Truly, You are the best Protector and the best to give victory, O Allah. Amn.

May Allah bestow His blessing and peace upon Prophet Muhammad and upon his family and companions.

APPENDIX I

Al-Wazifa al-Kubra

أعوذُ باللهِ السميعِ العليمِ مِنَ الشيطانِ الرجيمِ.

بِسْمِ اللهِ الرَّحْمَنِ الرَّحِيمِ
الْحَمْدُ لِلَّهِ رَبِّ الْعَالَمِينَ ﴿2﴾ الرَّحْمَنِ الرَّحِيمِ ﴿3﴾ مَالِكِ يَوْمِ الدِّينِ ﴿4﴾ إِيَّاكَ نَعْبُدُ وَإِيَّاكَ نَسْتَعِينُ ﴿5﴾ اهْدِنَا الصِّرَاطَ الْمُسْتَقِيمَ ﴿6﴾ صِرَاطَ الَّذِينَ أَنْعَمْتَ عَلَيْهِمْ غَيْرِ الْمَغْضُوبِ عَلَيْهِمْ وَلَا الضَّالِّينَ ﴿7﴾

الم ﴿1﴾ ذَلِكَ الْكِتَابُ لَا رَيْبَ فِيهِ هُدًى لِلْمُتَّقِينَ ﴿2﴾ الَّذِينَ يُؤْمِنُونَ بِالْغَيْبِ وَيُقِيمُونَ الصَّلَاةَ وَمِمَّا رَزَقْنَاهُمْ يُنْفِقُونَ ﴿3﴾ وَالَّذِينَ يُؤْمِنُونَ بِمَا أُنْزِلَ إِلَيْكَ وَمَا أُنْزِلَ مِنْ قَبْلِكَ وَبِالْآخِرَةِ هُمْ يُوقِنُونَ ﴿4﴾ أُولَئِكَ عَلَى هُدًى مِنْ رَبِّهِمْ وَأُولَئِكَ هُمُ الْمُفْلِحُونَ ﴿5﴾

اللَّهُ لَا إِلَهَ إِلَّا هُوَ الْحَيُّ الْقَيُّومُ لَا تَأْخُذُهُ سِنَةٌ وَلَا نَوْمٌ لَهُ مَا فِي السَّمَاوَاتِ وَمَا فِي الْأَرْضِ مَنْ ذَا الَّذِي يَشْفَعُ عِنْدَهُ إِلَّا بِإِذْنِهِ يَعْلَمُ مَا بَيْنَ أَيْدِيهِمْ وَمَا خَلْفَهُمْ وَلَا يُحِيطُونَ بِشَيْءٍ مِنْ عِلْمِهِ إِلَّا بِمَا شَاءَ وَسِعَ كُرْسِيُّهُ السَّمَاوَاتِ

وَالْأَرْضَ وَلَا يَئُودُهُ حِفْظُهُمَا وَهُوَ الْعَلِيُّ الْعَظِيمُ ﴿255﴾ لَا إِكْرَاهَ فِي الدِّينِ قَدْ تَبَيَّنَ الرُّشْدُ مِنَ الْغَيِّ فَمَنْ يَكْفُرْ بِالطَّاغُوتِ وَيُؤْمِنْ بِاللَّهِ فَقَدِ اسْتَمْسَكَ بِالْعُرْوَةِ الْوُثْقَىٰ لَا انْفِصَامَ لَهَا وَاللَّهُ سَمِيعٌ عَلِيمٌ ﴿256﴾ اللَّهُ وَلِيُّ الَّذِينَ آمَنُوا يُخْرِجُهُمْ مِنَ الظُّلُمَاتِ إِلَى النُّورِ وَالَّذِينَ كَفَرُوا أَوْلِيَاؤُهُمُ الطَّاغُوتُ يُخْرِجُونَهُمْ مِنَ النُّورِ إِلَى الظُّلُمَاتِ أُولَٰئِكَ أَصْحَابُ النَّارِ هُمْ فِيهَا خَالِدُونَ ﴿257﴾ لِلَّهِ مَا فِي السَّمَاوَاتِ وَمَا فِي الْأَرْضِ وَإِنْ تُبْدُوا مَا فِي أَنْفُسِكُمْ أَوْ تُخْفُوهُ يُحَاسِبْكُمْ بِهِ اللَّهُ فَيَغْفِرُ لِمَنْ يَشَاءُ وَيُعَذِّبُ مَنْ يَشَاءُ وَاللَّهُ عَلَىٰ كُلِّ شَيْءٍ قَدِيرٌ ﴿284﴾ آمَنَ الرَّسُولُ بِمَا أُنْزِلَ إِلَيْهِ مِنْ رَبِّهِ وَالْمُؤْمِنُونَ كُلٌّ آمَنَ بِاللَّهِ وَمَلَائِكَتِهِ وَكُتُبِهِ وَرُسُلِهِ لَا نُفَرِّقُ بَيْنَ أَحَدٍ مِنْ رُسُلِهِ وَقَالُوا سَمِعْنَا وَأَطَعْنَا غُفْرَانَكَ رَبَّنَا وَإِلَيْكَ الْمَصِيرُ ﴿285﴾ لَا يُكَلِّفُ اللَّهُ نَفْسًا إِلَّا وُسْعَهَا لَهَا مَا كَسَبَتْ وَعَلَيْهَا مَا اكْتَسَبَتْ رَبَّنَا لَا تُؤَاخِذْنَا إِنْ نَسِينَا أَوْ أَخْطَأْنَا رَبَّنَا وَلَا تَحْمِلْ عَلَيْنَا إِصْرًا كَمَا حَمَلْتَهُ عَلَى الَّذِينَ مِنْ قَبْلِنَا رَبَّنَا وَلَا تُحَمِّلْنَا مَا لَا طَاقَةَ لَنَا بِهِ وَاعْفُ عَنَّا وَاغْفِرْ لَنَا وَارْحَمْنَا أَنْتَ مَوْلَانَا فَانْصُرْنَا عَلَى الْقَوْمِ الْكَافِرِينَ ﴿286﴾

بِسْمِ اللَّهِ الرَّحْمَٰنِ الرَّحِيمِ
الم ﴿1﴾ اللَّهُ لَا إِلَٰهَ إِلَّا هُوَ الْحَيُّ الْقَيُّومُ ﴿2﴾

وَعَنَتِ الْوُجُوهُ لِلْحَيِّ الْقَيُّومِ وَقَدْ خَابَ مَنْ حَمَلَ ظُلْمًا ﴿111﴾ وَمَنْ يَعْمَلْ مِنَ الصَّالِحَاتِ وَهُوَ مُؤْمِنٌ فَلَا يَخَافُ ظُلْمًا وَلَا هَضْمًا ﴿112﴾

حَسْبِيَ اللَّهُ لَا إِلَٰهَ إِلَّا هُوَ عَلَيْهِ تَوَكَّلْتُ وَهُوَ رَبُّ الْعَرْشِ الْعَظِيمِ ﴿129﴾

قُلِ ادْعُوا اللَّهَ أَوِ ادْعُوا الرَّحْمَٰنَ أَيًّا مَا تَدْعُوا فَلَهُ الْأَسْمَاءُ الْحُسْنَىٰ وَلَا تَجْهَرْ بِصَلَاتِكَ وَلَا تُخَافِتْ بِهَا وَابْتَغِ بَيْنَ ذَٰلِكَ سَبِيلًا ﴿110﴾ وَقُلِ الْحَمْدُ لِلَّهِ الَّذِي لَمْ يَتَّخِذْ وَلَدًا وَلَمْ يَكُنْ لَهُ شَرِيكٌ فِي الْمُلْكِ وَلَمْ يَكُنْ لَهُ وَلِيٌّ مِنَ الذُّلِّ وَكَبِّرْهُ تَكْبِيرًا ﴿111﴾

أَفَحَسِبْتُمْ أَنَّمَا خَلَقْنَاكُمْ عَبَثًا وَأَنَّكُمْ إِلَيْنَا لَا تُرْجَعُونَ ﴿115﴾ فَتَعَالَى اللَّهُ الْمَلِكُ الْحَقُّ لَا إِلَٰهَ إِلَّا هُوَ رَبُّ الْعَرْشِ الْكَرِيمِ ﴿116﴾ وَمَنْ يَدْعُ مَعَ اللَّهِ إِلَٰهًا آخَرَ لَا بُرْهَانَ لَهُ بِهِ فَإِنَّمَا حِسَابُهُ عِنْدَ رَبِّهِ إِنَّهُ لَا يُفْلِحُ الْكَافِرُونَ ﴿117﴾ وَقُلْ رَبِّ اغْفِرْ وَارْحَمْ وَأَنْتَ خَيْرُ الرَّاحِمِينَ ﴿118﴾

فَسُبْحَانَ اللَّهِ حِينَ تُمْسُونَ وَحِينَ تُصْبِحُونَ ﴿17﴾ وَلَهُ الْحَمْدُ فِي السَّمَاوَاتِ وَالْأَرْضِ وَعَشِيًّا وَحِينَ تُظْهِرُونَ ﴿18﴾ يُخْرِجُ الْحَيَّ مِنَ الْمَيِّتِ وَيُخْرِجُ الْمَيِّتَ مِنَ الْحَيِّ وَيُحْيِي الْأَرْضَ بَعْدَ مَوْتِهَا وَكَذَٰلِكَ تُخْرَجُونَ ﴿19﴾ وَمِنْ آيَاتِهِ أَنْ خَلَقَكُمْ مِنْ تُرَابٍ ثُمَّ إِذَا أَنْتُمْ بَشَرٌ تَنْتَشِرُونَ ﴿20﴾ وَمِنْ آيَاتِهِ أَنْ خَلَقَ لَكُمْ مِنْ أَنْفُسِكُمْ أَزْوَاجًا لِتَسْكُنُوا إِلَيْهَا وَجَعَلَ بَيْنَكُمْ مَوَدَّةً وَرَحْمَةً إِنَّ فِي ذَٰلِكَ لَآيَاتٍ لِقَوْمٍ يَتَفَكَّرُونَ ﴿21﴾ وَمِنْ آيَاتِهِ خَلْقُ السَّمَاوَاتِ وَالْأَرْضِ وَاخْتِلَافُ أَلْسِنَتِكُمْ وَأَلْوَانِكُمْ إِنَّ فِي ذَٰلِكَ لَآيَاتٍ لِلْعَالِمِينَ ﴿22﴾ وَمِنْ آيَاتِهِ مَنَامُكُمْ بِاللَّيْلِ وَالنَّهَارِ وَابْتِغَاؤُكُمْ مِنْ

فَضْلِهِ إِنَّ فِي ذَٰلِكَ لَآيَاتٍ لِقَوْمٍ يَسْمَعُونَ ﴿23﴾ وَمِنْ آيَاتِهِ يُرِيكُمُ الْبَرْقَ خَوْفًا وَطَمَعًا وَيُنَزِّلُ مِنَ السَّمَاءِ مَاءً فَيُحْيِي بِهِ الْأَرْضَ بَعْدَ مَوْتِهَا إِنَّ فِي ذَٰلِكَ لَآيَاتٍ لِقَوْمٍ يَعْقِلُونَ ﴿24﴾ وَمِنْ آيَاتِهِ أَنْ تَقُومَ السَّمَاءُ وَالْأَرْضُ بِأَمْرِهِ ثُمَّ إِذَا دَعَاكُمْ دَعْوَةً مِنَ الْأَرْضِ إِذَا أَنْتُمْ تَخْرُجُونَ ﴿25﴾ وَلَهُ مَنْ فِي السَّمَاوَاتِ وَالْأَرْضِ كُلٌّ لَهُ قَانِتُونَ ﴿26﴾

بِسْمِ اللَّهِ الرَّحْمَٰنِ الرَّحِيمِ
حم ﴿1﴾ تَنْزِيلُ الْكِتَابِ مِنَ اللَّهِ الْعَزِيزِ الْعَلِيمِ ﴿2﴾ غَافِرِ الذَّنْبِ وَقَابِلِ التَّوْبِ شَدِيدِ الْعِقَابِ ذِي الطَّوْلِ لَا إِلَٰهَ إِلَّا هُوَ إِلَيْهِ الْمَصِيرُ ﴿3﴾

هُوَ اللَّهُ الَّذِي لَا إِلَٰهَ إِلَّا هُوَ عَالِمُ الْغَيْبِ وَالشَّهَادَةِ هُوَ الرَّحْمَٰنُ الرَّحِيمُ ﴿22﴾ هُوَ اللَّهُ الَّذِي لَا إِلَٰهَ إِلَّا هُوَ الْمَلِكُ الْقُدُّوسُ السَّلَامُ الْمُؤْمِنُ الْمُهَيْمِنُ الْعَزِيزُ الْجَبَّارُ الْمُتَكَبِّرُ سُبْحَانَ اللَّهِ عَمَّا يُشْرِكُونَ ﴿23﴾ هُوَ اللَّهُ الْخَالِقُ الْبَارِئُ الْمُصَوِّرُ لَهُ الْأَسْمَاءُ الْحُسْنَىٰ يُسَبِّحُ لَهُ مَا فِي السَّمَاوَاتِ وَالْأَرْضِ وَهُوَ الْعَزِيزُ الْحَكِيمُ ﴿24﴾

بِسْمِ اللَّهِ الرَّحْمَٰنِ الرَّحِيمِ
قُلْ يَا أَيُّهَا الْكَافِرُونَ ﴿1﴾ لَا أَعْبُدُ مَا تَعْبُدُونَ ﴿2﴾ وَلَا أَنْتُمْ عَابِدُونَ مَا أَعْبُدُ ﴿3﴾ وَلَا أَنَا عَابِدٌ مَا عَبَدْتُمْ ﴿4﴾ وَلَا أَنْتُمْ عَابِدُونَ مَا أَعْبُدُ ﴿5﴾ لَكُمْ دِينُكُمْ وَلِيَ دِينِ ﴿6﴾
بِسْمِ اللَّهِ الرَّحْمَٰنِ الرَّحِيمِ
إِذَا جَاءَ نَصْرُ اللَّهِ وَالْفَتْحُ ﴿1﴾ وَرَأَيْتَ النَّاسَ يَدْخُلُونَ فِي

دِينِ اللَّهِ أَفْوَاجًا ﴿2﴾ فَسَبِّحْ بِحَمْدِ رَبِّكَ وَاسْتَغْفِرْهُ إِنَّهُ كَانَ تَوَّابًا ﴿3﴾

بِسْمِ اللهِ الرَّحْمَنِ الرَّحِيمِ
قُلْ هُوَ اللَّهُ أَحَدٌ ﴿1﴾ اللَّهُ الصَّمَدُ ﴿2﴾ لَمْ يَلِدْ وَلَمْ يُولَدْ ﴿3﴾ وَلَمْ يَكُنْ لَهُ كُفُوًا أَحَدٌ ﴿4﴾

بِسْمِ اللهِ الرَّحْمَنِ الرَّحِيمِ
قُلْ أَعُوذُ بِرَبِّ الْفَلَقِ ﴿1﴾ مِنْ شَرِّ مَا خَلَقَ ﴿2﴾ وَمِنْ شَرِّ غَاسِقٍ إِذَا وَقَبَ ﴿3﴾ وَمِنْ شَرِّ النَّفَّاثَاتِ فِي الْعُقَدِ ﴿4﴾ وَمِنْ شَرِّ حَاسِدٍ إِذَا حَسَدَ ﴿5﴾

بِسْمِ اللهِ الرَّحْمَنِ الرَّحِيمِ
قُلْ أَعُوذُ بِرَبِّ النَّاسِ ﴿1﴾ مَلِكِ النَّاسِ ﴿2﴾ إِلَهِ النَّاسِ ﴿3﴾ مِنْ شَرِّ الْوَسْوَاسِ الْخَنَّاسِ ﴿4﴾ الَّذِي يُوَسْوِسُ فِي صُدُورِ النَّاسِ ﴿5﴾ مِنَ الْجِنَّةِ وَالنَّاسِ ﴿6﴾

أَصْبَحْنَـا وَأَصْبَحَ الْمُلْكُ لِلَّـهِ، وَالْحَمْدُ لِلَّهِ كُلُّهُ لِلَّهِ عَزَّ وَجَلَّ، لَا شَرِيكَ لَهُ، لَا إِلَهَ إِلَّا اللَّهُ، وَإِلَيْهِ النُّشُورُ. (ثلاثاً)

أَصْبَحْنَا عَلى فِطْرَةِ الإِسْلامِ، وَكَلِمَةِ الإِخْلاصِ، وَدِينِ نَبِيِّنَا محمَّدٍ صَلَّى اللهُ عليه وسلَّمَ، وعلى مِلَّةِ أَبِينا إِبراهيمَ، حَنِيفًا مُسْلِمًا، وما كان مِنَ المُشرِكينَ. (ثلاثاً)

اللَّهُمَّ إِنِّي أَصْبَحْتُ مِنكَ في نِعمةٍ وعافيةٍ وسِترٍ، فَأَتِمَّمْ عليَّ نِعمتَكَ وعافِيَتَكَ وسِترَكَ في الدُّنيا والآخِرة. (ثلاثاً)

اللَّهُمَّ ما أَصْبَحَ بي مِن نِعمةٍ، أَوْ بِأَحدٍ مِن خَلقِكَ، فَمِنكَ وحدَكَ لا شريكَ لكَ، فَلَكَ الحمدُ، ولكَ الشُّكرُ. (ثلاثاً)

يا ربِّ! لَكَ الحمدُ كما يَنبغي لِجلالِ وجهِكَ، ولِعظيمِ سُلطانِكَ. (ثلاثاً)

رَضيتُ باللَّهِ ربًّا، وبالإِسلامِ دينًا، وبمحمَّدٍ نبيًّا. (ثلاثاً)

سُبْحَانَ اللهِ وَبِحَمْدِهِ، عَدَدَ خَلْقِهِ، وَرِضَا نَفْسِهِ، وَزِنَةَ عَرْشِهِ، وَمِدَادَ كَلِمَاتِهِ. (ثلاثاً)

بِسمِ اللهِ الذي لا يَضرُّ مع اسمِهِ شيءٌ في الأرضِ ولا في السَّماءِ وهو السَّميعُ العليمُ. (ثلاثاً)

اللَّهُمَّ إِنَّا نَعوذُ بكَ مِن أَنْ نُشرِكَ بكَ شيئًا نَعلَمُهُ،

وَنَسْتَغْفِرُكَ لِمَا لَا نَعْلَمُ. (ثلاثاً)

أَعُوذُ بِكَلِمَاتِ اللهِ التَّامَّاتِ مِنْ شَرِّ مَا خَلَقَ. (ثلاثاً)

اللَّهُمَّ إِنِّي أَعُوذُ بِكَ مِنَ الهَمِّ والحَزَنِ، والعَجْزِ والكَسَلِ، والجُبْنِ والبُخْلِ، وضَلَعِ الدَّيْنِ، وغَلَبَةِ الرِّجَالِ. (ثلاثاً)

اللهمَّ عَافِنِي فِي بَدَنِي، اللهمَّ عَافِنِي فِي سَمْعِي،
اللهمَّ عَافِنِي فِي بَصَرِي، اللهمَّ إِنِّي أَعُوذُ بِكَ مِنَ الكُفْرِ والفَقْرِ،
اللهمَّ إِنِّي أَعُوذُ بِكَ مِنْ عَذَابِ القَبْرِ، لَا إِلَهَ إِلَّا أَنْتَ. (ثلاثاً)

اللهمَّ إِنِّي أَعُوذُ بِكَ مِنَ الكُفْرِ والفَقْرِ،
اللهمَّ إِنِّي أَعُوذُ بِكَ مِنْ عَذَابِ القَبْرِ، لَا إِلَهَ إِلَّا أَنْتَ. (ثلاثاً)

اللَّهُمَّ أَنْتَ رَبِّي، لَا إِلَهَ إِلَّا أَنْتَ، خَلَقْتَنِي وَأَنَا عَبْدُكَ، وَأَنَا عَلَى عَهْدِكَ وَوَعْدِكَ مَا اسْتَطَعْتُ، أَبُوءُ لَكَ بِنِعْمَتِكَ عَلَيَّ، وَأَبُوءُ لَكَ بِذَنْبِي فَاغْفِرْ لِي، فَإِنَّهُ لَا يَغْفِرُ الذُّنُوبَ إِلَّا أَنْتَ. (ثلاثاً)

أَسْتَغْفِرُ اللَّهَ الَّذِي لَا إِلَهَ إِلَّا هُوَ الحَيُّ القَيُّومُ وَأَتُوبُ إِلَيْهِ. (ثلاثاً)

اللَّهُمَّ صَلِّ عَلَى مُحَمَّدٍ، وَعَلَى آلِ مُحَمَّدٍ، كَمَا صَلَّيْتَ عَلَى إِبْرَاهِيمَ، وَعَلَى آلِ إِبْرَاهِيمَ، إِنَّكَ حَمِيدٌ مَجِيدٌ، وَبَارِكْ عَلَى مُحَمَّدٍ، وَعَلَى آلِ مُحَمَّدٍ، كَمَا بَارَكْتَ عَلَى إِبْرَاهِيمَ، وَعَلَى آلِ إِبْرَاهِيمَ، فِي العَالَمِينَ إِنَّكَ حَمِيدٌ مَجِيدٌ. (ثلاثاً)

سُبْحَانَ اللهِ، وَالْحَمْدُ لِلّهِ، وَلَا إِلَهَ إِلَّا اللهُ، وَاللهُ أَكْبَرُ. (ثلاثاً)

لا إِلَهَ إِلَّا اللهُ وحْدَهُ لا شَرِيكَ له،
له المُلْكُ وله الحَمْدُ، وهو عَلَى كُلِّ شيءٍ قَدِيرٌ. (ثلاثاً)

سبحانَكَ اللّهمَّ وبحمدِكَ أشهدُ أن
لا إلَهَ إلَّا أنتَ أستغفرُكَ وأتوبُ إليكَ. (ثلاثاً)

اللهمَّ صلِّ وسلِّمْ وبارِكْ على سيِّدنا محمَّد، عبدِك ونبيِّك ورسولِك النبيِّ الأُمِّي، وعلى آلهِ وصحْبهِ وسلِّمْ تسليمًا؛ عددَ ما أحاط به علمُكَ، وخطَّ به قلمُكَ، وأحصاه كتابُكَ، وارضَ اللهمَّ عن سادتِنا أبي بكرٍ وعمر، وعثمانَ وعلي، وعن الصحابةِ أجمعين، وعن التابعين وتابعيهم بإحسانٍ إلى يوم الدِّين.

سُبْحَانَ رَبِّكَ رَبِّ العِزَّةِ عَمَّا يَصِفُونَ
وَسَلَامٌ عَلَى المُرْسَلِينَ وَالحَمْدُ لِلَّهِ رَبِّ العَالَمِينَ

APPENDIX II
Al-Wazifa al-Sughra

أعوذُ باللهِ السميعِ العليم مِنَ الشيطانِ الرجيم.

بِسْمِ اللهِ الرَّحْمَنِ الرَّحِيمِ
الْحَمْدُ لِلَّهِ رَبِّ الْعَالَمِينَ ﴿2﴾ الرَّحْمَنِ الرَّحِيمِ ﴿3﴾ مَالِكِ يَوْمِ الدِّينِ ﴿4﴾ إِيَّاكَ نَعْبُدُ وَإِيَّاكَ نَسْتَعِينُ ﴿5﴾ اهْدِنَا الصِّرَاطَ الْمُسْتَقِيمَ ﴿6﴾ صِرَاطَ الَّذِينَ أَنْعَمْتَ عَلَيْهِمْ غَيْرِ الْمَغْضُوبِ عَلَيْهِمْ وَلَا الضَّالِّينَ ﴿7﴾

بِسْمِ اللهِ الرَّحْمَنِ الرَّحِيمِ
الم ﴿1﴾ ذَلِكَ الْكِتَابُ لَا رَيْبَ فِيهِ هُدًى لِلْمُتَّقِينَ ﴿2﴾ الَّذِينَ يُؤْمِنُونَ بِالْغَيْبِ وَيُقِيمُونَ الصَّلَاةَ وَمِمَّا رَزَقْنَاهُمْ يُنْفِقُونَ ﴿3﴾ وَالَّذِينَ يُؤْمِنُونَ بِمَا أُنْزِلَ إِلَيْكَ وَمَا أُنْزِلَ مِنْ قَبْلِكَ وَبِالْآخِرَةِ هُمْ يُوقِنُونَ ﴿4﴾ أُولَئِكَ عَلَى هُدًى مِنْ رَبِّهِمْ وَأُولَئِكَ هُمُ الْمُفْلِحُونَ ﴿5﴾

اللَّهُ لَا إِلَهَ إِلَّا هُوَ الْحَيُّ الْقَيُّومُ لَا تَأْخُذُهُ سِنَةٌ وَلَا نَوْمٌ لَهُ مَا فِي السَّمَاوَاتِ وَمَا فِي الْأَرْضِ مَنْ ذَا الَّذِي يَشْفَعُ عِنْدَهُ إِلَّا بِإِذْنِهِ يَعْلَمُ مَا بَيْنَ أَيْدِيهِمْ وَمَا خَلْفَهُمْ وَلَا يُحِيطُونَ بِشَيْءٍ

مِنْ عِلْمِهِ إِلَّا بِمَا شَاءَ وَسِعَ كُرْسِيُّهُ السَّمَاوَاتِ وَالْأَرْضَ وَلَا يَئُودُهُ حِفْظُهُمَا وَهُوَ الْعَلِيُّ الْعَظِيمُ ﴿255﴾ لَا إِكْرَاهَ فِي الدِّينِ قَدْ تَبَيَّنَ الرُّشْدُ مِنَ الْغَيِّ فَمَنْ يَكْفُرْ بِالطَّاغُوتِ وَيُؤْمِنْ بِاللَّهِ فَقَدِ اسْتَمْسَكَ بِالْعُرْوَةِ الْوُثْقَىٰ لَا انْفِصَامَ لَهَا وَاللَّهُ سَمِيعٌ عَلِيمٌ ﴿256﴾ اللَّهُ وَلِيُّ الَّذِينَ آمَنُوا يُخْرِجُهُمْ مِنَ الظُّلُمَاتِ إِلَى النُّورِ وَالَّذِينَ كَفَرُوا أَوْلِيَاؤُهُمُ الطَّاغُوتُ يُخْرِجُونَهُمْ مِنَ النُّورِ إِلَى الظُّلُمَاتِ أُولَٰئِكَ أَصْحَابُ النَّارِ هُمْ فِيهَا خَالِدُونَ ﴿257﴾

لِلَّهِ مَا فِي السَّمَاوَاتِ وَمَا فِي الْأَرْضِ وَإِنْ تُبْدُوا مَا فِي أَنْفُسِكُمْ أَوْ تُخْفُوهُ يُحَاسِبْكُمْ بِهِ اللَّهُ فَيَغْفِرُ لِمَنْ يَشَاءُ وَيُعَذِّبُ مَنْ يَشَاءُ وَاللَّهُ عَلَىٰ كُلِّ شَيْءٍ قَدِيرٌ ﴿284﴾ آمَنَ الرَّسُولُ بِمَا أُنْزِلَ إِلَيْهِ مِنْ رَبِّهِ وَالْمُؤْمِنُونَ كُلٌّ آمَنَ بِاللَّهِ وَمَلَائِكَتِهِ وَكُتُبِهِ وَرُسُلِهِ لَا نُفَرِّقُ بَيْنَ أَحَدٍ مِنْ رُسُلِهِ وَقَالُوا سَمِعْنَا وَأَطَعْنَا غُفْرَانَكَ رَبَّنَا وَإِلَيْكَ الْمَصِيرُ ﴿285﴾ لَا يُكَلِّفُ اللَّهُ نَفْسًا إِلَّا وُسْعَهَا لَهَا مَا كَسَبَتْ وَعَلَيْهَا مَا اكْتَسَبَتْ رَبَّنَا لَا تُؤَاخِذْنَا إِنْ نَسِينَا أَوْ أَخْطَأْنَا رَبَّنَا وَلَا تَحْمِلْ عَلَيْنَا إِصْرًا كَمَا حَمَلْتَهُ عَلَى الَّذِينَ مِنْ قَبْلِنَا رَبَّنَا وَلَا تُحَمِّلْنَا مَا لَا طَاقَةَ لَنَا بِهِ وَاعْفُ عَنَّا وَاغْفِرْ لَنَا وَارْحَمْنَا أَنْتَ مَوْلَانَا فَانْصُرْنَا عَلَى الْقَوْمِ الْكَافِرِينَ ﴿286﴾

بِسْمِ اللَّهِ الرَّحْمَٰنِ الرَّحِيمِ
قُلْ هُوَ اللَّهُ أَحَدٌ ﴿1﴾ اللَّهُ الصَّمَدُ ﴿2﴾ لَمْ يَلِدْ وَلَمْ يُولَدْ ﴿3﴾ وَلَمْ يَكُنْ لَهُ كُفُوًا أَحَدٌ ﴿4﴾

(ثلاثًا)

بِسْمِ اللَّهِ الرَّحْمَنِ الرَّحِيمِ
قُلْ أَعُوذُ بِرَبِّ الْفَلَقِ ﴿1﴾ مِنْ شَرِّ مَا خَلَقَ ﴿2﴾ وَمِنْ شَرِّ غَاسِقٍ إِذَا وَقَبَ ﴿3﴾ وَمِنْ شَرِّ النَّفَّاثَاتِ فِي الْعُقَدِ ﴿4﴾ وَمِنْ شَرِّ حَاسِدٍ إِذَا حَسَدَ ﴿5﴾

(ثلاثًا)

بِسْمِ اللَّهِ الرَّحْمَنِ الرَّحِيمِ
قُلْ أَعُوذُ بِرَبِّ النَّاسِ ﴿1﴾ مَلِكِ النَّاسِ ﴿2﴾ إِلَهِ النَّاسِ ﴿3﴾ مِنْ شَرِّ الْوَسْوَاسِ الْخَنَّاسِ ﴿4﴾ الَّذِي يُوَسْوِسُ فِي صُدُورِ النَّاسِ ﴿5﴾ مِنَ الْجِنَّةِ وَالنَّاسِ ﴿6﴾

أَصْبَحْنَا وَأَصْبَحَ الْمُلْكُ لِلَّهِ، وَالْحَمْدُ كُلُّهُ لِلَّهِ عَزَّ وَجَلَّ، لَا شَرِيكَ لَهُ، لَا إِلَهَ إِلَّا اللَّهُ، وَإِلَيْهِ النُّشُورُ. (ثلاثًا)

أَصْبَحْنَا عَلَى فِطْرَةِ الْإِسْلَامِ، وَكَلِمَةِ الْإِخْلَاصِ، وَدِينِ نَبِيِّنَا مُحَمَّدٍ صَلَّى اللَّهُ عَلَيْهِ وَسَلَّمَ، وَعَلَى مِلَّةِ أَبِينَا إِبْرَاهِيمَ، حَنِيفًا مُسْلِمًا، وَمَا كَانَ مِنَ الْمُشْرِكِينَ. (ثلاثًا)

اللَّهُمَّ إِنِّي أَصْبَحْتُ مِنْكَ فِي نِعْمَةٍ وَعَافِيَةٍ وَسِتْرٍ، فَأَتْمِمْ عَلَيَّ نِعْمَتَكَ وَعَافِيَتَكَ وَسِتْرَكَ فِي الدُّنْيَا وَالْآخِرَةِ. (ثلاثًا)

اللَّهُمَّ مَا أَصْبَحَ بِي مِنْ نِعْمَةٍ، أَوْ بِأَحَدٍ مِنْ خَلْقِكَ، فَمِنْكَ وَحْدَكَ لَا شَرِيكَ لَكَ، فَلَكَ الْحَمْدُ، وَلَكَ الشُّكْرُ. (ثلاثًا)

يَا رَبِّ! لَكَ الْحَمْدُ كَمَا يَنْبَغِي لِجَلَالِ وَجْهِكَ، وَلِعَظِيمِ سُلْطَانِكَ. (ثلاثًا)

رَضِيتُ بِاللَّهِ رَبًّا، وَبِالْإِسْلَامِ دِينًا، وَبِمُحَمَّدٍ نَبِيًّا. (ثلاثًا)

بِسْمِ اللَّهِ الَّذِي لَا يَضُرُّ مَعَ اسْمِهِ شَيْءٌ فِي الْأَرْضِ وَلَا فِي السَّمَاءِ وَهُوَ السَّمِيعُ الْعَلِيمُ. (ثلاثًا)

اللَّهُمَّ إِنَّا نَعُوذُ بِكَ مِنْ أَنْ نُشْرِكَ بِكَ شَيْئًا نَعْلَمُهُ، وَنَسْتَغْفِرُكَ لِمَا لَا نَعْلَمُ. (ثلاثًا)

أَعُوذُ بِكَلِمَاتِ اللَّهِ التَّامَّاتِ مِنْ شَرِّ مَا خَلَقَ. (ثلاثًا)

اللَّهُمَّ إِنِّي أَعُوذُ بِكَ مِنَ الهَمِّ والحَزَنِ، والعَجزِ والكَسَلِ، والجُبْنِ والبُخْلِ، وضَلَعِ الدَّيْنِ، وغَلَبَةِ الرِّجالِ. (ثلاثاً)

اللهمَّ عافِني في بدَني، اللهمَّ عافِني في سمعي،
اللهمَّ عافِني في بصري. (ثلاثاً)

اللهـمَّ إِنِّي أعوذُ بِكَ مِنَ الكفرِ والفقرِ،
اللهـمَّ إِنِّي أعـوذُ بِكَ مِنْ عذابِ القبرِ، لا إلهَ إلَّا أنتَ. (ثلاثاً)

اللَّهُمَّ أَنْتَ رَبِّي، لا إلَهَ إلَّا أنْتَ، خَلَقْتَنِي وأنا عَبْدُكَ، وأنا على عَهْدِكَ وَوَعْدِكَ ما اسْتَطَعْتُ، أَبُوءُ لَكَ بِنِعْمَتِكَ عَلَيَّ، وأَبُوءُ لَكَ بِذَنْبِي فاغْفِرْ لِي، فإنَّه لا يَغْفِرُ الذُّنُوبَ إلَّا أَنْتَ. (ثلاثاً)

اللَّهُمَّ صَلِّ عَلَى مُحَمَّدٍ، وَعَلَى آلِ مُحَمَّدٍ، كَمَا صَلَّيْتَ عَلَى إِبْرَاهِيمَ، وَعَلَى آلِ إِبْرَاهِيمَ، إِنَّكَ حَمِيدٌ مَجِيدٌ، وَبَارِكْ عَلَى مُحَمَّدٍ، وَعَلَى آلِ مُحَمَّدٍ، كَمَا بَارَكْتَ عَلَى إِبْرَاهِيمَ، وَعَلَى آلِ إِبْرَاهِيمَ، فِي العَالَمِينَ إِنَّكَ حَمِيدٌ مَجِيدٌ. (عشراً)

سُبْحَانَ اللهِ، وَالْحَمْدُ لِلَّهِ، وَلَا إِلَهَ إِلَّا اللهُ، وَاللهُ أَكْبَرُ. (مائة)

لا إلَهَ إلَّا اللَّهُ وحْدَهُ لا شَرِيكَ له،
لـه المُلْكُ وله الحَمْدُ، وهو عَلَى كُلِّ شيءٍ قَدِيرٌ. (عشراً)

سبحانَكَ اللهمَّ وبحمدِكَ أشهدُ أن
لا إلهَ إلَّا أنتَ أستغفرُكَ وأتوبُ إليكَ. (ثلاثاً)

اللهمّ صلِّ وسلِّمْ وبارِكْ على سيِّدنا محمَّد، عبدك ونبيِّك ورسولك النبيُّ الأُمِّي، وعلى آله وصحبه وسلِّمْ تسليمًا؛ عددَ ما أحاط به علمُك، وخطَّ به قلمُك، وأحصاه كتابُك، وارضَ اللهمّ عن سادتِنا أبي بكر وعمر، وعثمان وعلي، وعن الصحابة أجمعين، وعن التابعين وتابعيهم بإحسانٍ إلى يوم الدّين.

سُبْحَانَ رَبِّكَ رَبِّ الْعِزَّةِ عَمَّا يَصِفُونَ
وَسَلَامٌ عَلَى الْمُرْسَلِينَ وَالْحَمْدُ لِلَّهِ رَبِّ الْعَالَمِينَ

APPENDIX III
Wird al-Rabita

قُلِ اللَّهُمَّ مَالِكَ الْمُلْكِ تُؤْتِي الْمُلْكَ مَنْ تَشَاءُ وَتَنْزِعُ الْمُلْكَ مِمَّنْ تَشَاءُ وَتُعِزُّ مَنْ تَشَاءُ وَتُذِلُّ مَنْ تَشَاءُ بِيَدِكَ الْخَيْرُ إِنَّكَ عَلَىٰ كُلِّ شَيْءٍ قَدِيرٌ ﴿26﴾ تُولِجُ اللَّيْلَ فِي النَّهَارِ وَتُولِجُ النَّهَارَ فِي اللَّيْلِ وَتُخْرِجُ الْحَيَّ مِنَ الْمَيِّتِ وَتُخْرِجُ الْمَيِّتَ مِنَ الْحَيِّ وَتَرْزُقُ مَنْ تَشَاءُ بِغَيْرِ حِسَابٍ ﴿27﴾

(ثم يتلوا الدعاء المأثور بعد ذلك)
اللَّهُمَّ إنَّ هذا إقبالُ ليلِك وإدبارُ نهارِك وأصواتُ دعاتِك فاغفر لي

(ثم يستحضر صورة من يعرفم ن إخوانه في ذهنه ويستشعر الصلة الروحية بينه وبين من لم يعرفه منهم، ثم يدعو لهم مثل هذا الدعاء)
اللهم إنك تعلم أن هذه القلوب قد اجتمعت على محبتك، والتقت على طاعتك وتوحدت على دعوتك، وتعاهدت على نصرت شريعتك. فوثق اللهم رابطتها وآدام ودها، وأهداها سبلها وأملئها بنورك الذي لا يخبو. واشرح صدورها بفيض الإيمان بك وجميل التوكل عليك، وأحيها بمعرفتك، وأمتها على الشهادة في سبيلك، إنك نعم المولى ونعم النصير. اللهم آمين. وصل اللهم على سيدنا محمد وعلى آله وصحبه وسلّم.

ALSO AVAILABLE BY LIGHT PUBLISHING

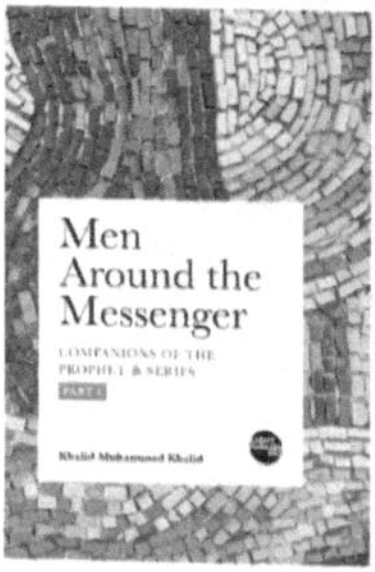

www.ingramcontent.com/pod-product-compliance
Lightning Source LLC
Chambersburg PA
CBHW011959090526
44590CB00023B/3782